JAMES DEAN

REVISITED

DENNIS STOCK

JAMES DEAN
REVISITED

CHRONICLE
BOOKS

SAN FRANCISCO

First published by Chronicle Books in 1987

Copyright © 1986 by Dennis Stock and Schirmer/Mosel,
München. All rights reserved. No part of this book may
be reproduced in any form without written permission
from the publisher.
English translation copyright © 1986 by Plexus
Publishing Limited.
Printed and bound in Japan
Library of Congress Cataloging in Publication Data
available.

ISBN: 0-87701-471-X

10   9   8   7   6   5   4   3   2   1

Chronicle Books
San Francisco, California

Design: Woods + Woods Graphic Communications

INTRODUCTION

Fairmount, Indiana, 1955

After the death of my friend James Dean, few illusions about the paradise of Hollywood remained. In the face of the reality of his austere funeral, all fantasies attached to the world of stars were greatly reduced.

Lew Bracker and I had arrived late at the simple brick Quaker church in Fairmount. Family and friends were already seated in the straight-backed pews. At the head of the center aisle, in front of the altar, lay the closed coffin, bedecked with flowers. For all I knew, it was the same coffin he had foolishly posed in a few months before. The organ played "Goin' Home." We found seats finally in the front row to the left of the altar. I immediately saw gentle Marcus Winslow, Jimmy's uncle. The family sat diagonally across from the coffin. Our eyes met often, and we had great difficulty choking back the sobs of pain we shared. It had been less than eight months since my last visit to Fairmount, with Jimmy, when I had had the pleasure of staying with the family as I photographed and pursued Jimmy's origins. We had hit it off exceptionally well, for the Winslows were extremely open and gracious. It seemed so wrong that this decent, generous family had to suffer this untimely loss. As surrogate parents, their devotion to Jimmy's upbringing was complete, their love unlimited.

I don't remember the eulogies; the wounds of loss blurred most of what was said. The service completed, the family filed out to receive the condolences of Fairmount friends. Hesitantly, I approached Marcus and we fell into each other's arms. "Boy, where have you been?" His face was tear-drenched and desperate. His wife, Ortense, admonished me for not having contacted them sooner, but was grateful that I had been the catalyst in releasing Marcus's repressed feelings. He had been silent since the notification of Jimmy's death. Marcus, the farmer, and Dennis, the city slicker, were as close as two people could get at that moment. Our mutual love of Jimmy and respect for each other helped to alleviate our devastation. My fondness for the Winslows remains intact to this day.

When I look back at Los Angeles in the early fifties, and specifically Sunset Boulevard, it reminds me of the board game in which you try to move clockwise and upward, past designated obstacles, into "Stardom and Wealth." Rolling the dice at the start, as a visitor on Mexican downtown Alvaro Street, the player inches past the pastel bungalows of Old Hollywood. With many other aspirants, we come to a holding pattern at the crossroads of Crescent Heights and Sunset. This intersection marks the beginning of the infamous Sunset Strip. If the dice were good, the roller continued and was hurled into the status-filled setting of Beverly Hills. A jump or two more and the ultimate was at hand: a sunset-bathed beach house. This road was literally and figuratively bumpy, curved and highly deceptive. As in real life, few players reach the Pacific enclave of the stars. Those who do are usually badly scarred and bruised.

The Sunset Strip in the fifties (I doubt if it has changed much) was the battlefield for those who needed to conquer Hollywood. In this two-mile area of nightclubs, restaurants, strip joints, and agents' offices the struggle for recognition was fought. Starlets, directors, producers, and actors elbowed one another for the space of two brief lines in the trade gossip columns. The establishments on the strip thrived on the anxiety of the fame-seekers, catering to the illusion of success; the prices were high, the façades ornate. Waiting at the foot of the strip for their turn were contestants who lived in the romantic hotels and cottages of the bygone twenties.

Those who arrived from the disciplines of the Broadway environment tried to make as gentle a transition into Hollywood as possible. They lived in the symbolic settings of the Chaplin and Keaton era, the Château Marmont and the Garden of Allah. The aging bungalows and suites insulated the ambivalent seekers from the East. The coffee shops, diners, and drug-stores were commandeered by the less affluent and served as social centers for the New York crowd. It was in this surreal, intense atmosphere that I met James Dean for the first time.

As an already established photojournalist in Hollywood, I had access to stars and movie events. On Sundays it was customary for Nicholas Ray, the director, to hold soirées at his bungalow in the grounds of the Château Marmont. Nick, an East Coast maverick, did not host singularly social affairs but rather offered the opportunity for talented people to meet weekly, exchange ideas, and form new ties. People from every part of the film industry converged on his little white bungalow on Sunday afternoons in the winter of '54–'55. The jugs of wine and the heated discussions somewhat reduced the superficiality that we experienced the rest of the week on the sound stages and in the offices of Hollywood.

Amid the animation of gesturing hands and passionate discussions, I stood somewhat removed and shy; like most photographers, one foot in and one foot out. Nick noticed my reserved appearance and led me up the small flight of stairs to a corner where a young man reclined, in a mood that seemed similar to mine.

We both awoke to the moment of our host's gracious introductions. I, the photographer, was presented to James Dean, the actor, and with that, Nick departed. There was nothing terribly imposing about this bespectacled young man. At first, his responses to my brief inquiries and observations were monosyllabic. But as the wine flowed more abundantly, so did our conversation. Relaxed, Jimmy asked about different aspects of photographic techniques, and I happily answered as best I could. Inevitably the conversation touched on his work, and on his most recent job. In a casual way he mentioned having completed a film with Elia Kazan called *East of Eden*; I looked blank, for I had neither read the book nor heard trade rumors about the production. We didn't pursue the film any further, but shortly before our conversation ended Jimmy invited me to attend a sneak preview of *East of Eden* the following Wednesday at a Santa Monica theater. With a nod and an "I'll see you there," we parted.

Midweek, I went to the shabby neighborhood movie house, totally unprepared for an experience that initiated a major chapter in my life. Jimmy's unassuming manner at Nick's had ill prepared me for the brilliant performance I watched that night in *East of Eden*.

There are ailments that medicine will never cure. During adolescence feelings are uniquely intense and repressed, and we ache with inarticulation and emotional frustrations. The teenager wrestles for years with the "need to be understood." It is a logical challenge along the course to individuality. The searching society seeks symbols that universalize experience. The artist seeks order, instinctively, and often crystallizes through gesture or deed a universal truth. His perception reaches the very heart of our common experience, and identification is immediate for the viewer. We then acknowledge the brilliance of the symbol. This is art, and the rarity of universal art makes James Dean's first major film performance all the more extraordinary. In *East of Eden*, as young Cal, who struggles to communicate with an intransigent father he loves, Dean expressed hues and shadings of adolescence that had probably never been seen before. I and the movie audience clearly empathized with Cal as Dean led us masterfully through his plight of alienation and innocence. Capitalizing on the limits of the adolescent's ability to articulate, Dean used his body to the utmost. His expressions were exceptionally graphic. Literally on the edge of my seat throughout the screening, I mentally photographed his rich variety of powerful gestures.

There was no question that a star was born with the first public screening of *East of Eden*, for the entire audience applauded loudly as the house lights signaled the end. It took a few moments for me to reconcile the image of Cal with that of the unimposing, reserved young man of the previous Sunday night. What I knew was that I had to do a story on James Dean. Out on the street, I searched for Jimmy to congratulate him and to arrange for an early meeting to discuss the possibilities of a photo-essay. In the alley on the side of the theater I found Jimmy seated on his motorcycle. He peered through his glasses at the crowds of newly acquired admirers; at this distance he could observe without being observed. Jimmy must have sensed his triumph, for as I approached, he burst into a big grin and said, "What do you think?" Since I was still deeply enveloped in the film I simply blurted, "You are an outstanding actor!" We were interrupted by friends congratulating Jimmy, and I suggested we meet the following morning for breakfast.

Let me try to explain my own position and attitude as a young man in Hollywood in those days. My contacts with New York magazines were well known to many publicity-seeking actors and agents, so I had ample opportunity to meet as many famous and creative people as I wanted. And though I greatly enjoyed being in the presence of recognized creative people, I was also aware that the relationship could be parasitical if I did not photograph in meaningful ways but simply relaxed with the exclusive opportunities I had to cover stars and up-and-coming stars. Dull photographs of famous people often are acclaimed primarily because of the status of the subject, so I tried to pursue themes that were best stated by a multiple-picture essay. In each assignment I searched for depth and meaning. It made the possibility of an exceptional photograph more frequent. If the photograph was good in spite of the subject, I felt I had succeeded.

Breakfast took place at Googie's, on the Strip, one of Jimmy's favorite hangouts. The coffee shop was packed, as usual, with unemployed actors and actresses, exchanging trade gossip and reading *Variety* in search of leads to film castings. Jimmy arrived at nine, sat down, and before our conversation could begin, he was surrounded by admirers. The exceptional success of the previous night's "sneak" was the topic of conversation throughout the restaurant. For two hours Jimmy reigned supreme. Acquaintances tried to ingratiate themselves with exaggerated compliments as they jockeyed for a closer friendship with the rising star. My patience was running thin, and I indicated I was going to leave, since there was no chance to talk. In one swift move Jimmy leaped from our booth, paid the bill, and led me to his motorcycle in the parking lot. "Get on; let's go up into the hills. My agent's got a place up there with a beautiful view, and we can talk." Since I'd never ridden on a motorcycle, I mounted the Triumph with trepidation, and with the realization that I was being tested. It was the first of my tests. We sped up the winding roads of Laurel Canyon, my arms securely wrapped around Jimmy's waist. We leaned wildly at each curve in the road. I tightened my grip around Jimmy's heavy leather jacket and screamed above the roaring motor, "If I go, you go!" Finally we slowed down as we reached the section of the dry Hollywood hills where Dick Clayton's house was. Stretched below us was a goodly portion of Los Angeles, and, in the far distance, the Pacific. On the bare ground we sat and talked for five hours.

There was no question that our meeting was investigatory in nature. Sparingly, Jimmy volunteered information about his background, and I elaborated on my qualifications and credentials. His awareness of my friendship with Humphrey Bogart and my membership in the elite photo agency Magnum helped to further the idea of a collaboration. My intent was solely to lead the conversation back to Jimmy's past so that I could start to formulate an outline of situations that we could visit and document with the camera. The story, as I explained it, was to reveal the environments that affected and shaped the unique character of James Byron Dean. We felt a trip to his hometown, Fairmount, Indiana, and to New York, the place of his professional beginnings, would best reveal those influences. We agreed to a trip to both those locales in the not-too-distant future. As was customary in my business, I would solicit an assignment guarantee to cover expenses. The obvious magazine to approach was *LIFE*. If I was assigned by the *LIFE* editors, we could set up a schedule for visiting Indiana and New York. We further agreed that I would have the first exclusive rights to a picture story on Jimmy.

It took only a week for *LIFE* to approve the assignment. I notified Jimmy, and we tentatively set our departure for Indiana and New York for two weeks hence. Meanwhile, I made a point of socializing a great deal with Jimmy, for the more I knew about his moods, the easier it would be to anticipate gestures and situations. By now there was an ever-increasing interest in the new star as the press became more and more aware of *East of Eden*. The upshot of Jimmy's increasing popularity was

reflected in the new stipulations he tried to enforce on the *LIFE* coverage. At one point he insisted on a cover guarantee and the hiring of a friend of his to write the text. It was an unusual and highly egocentric gesture. I said I'd pass the request on to the editors. It was a foolhardy demand, which I never conveyed to the magazine, gambling on our growing friendship to keep the assignment afloat. I told Jimmy the editor's answer was no. For days he acted like a spoiled kid, and then finally came around, making it possible for us to leave for Fairmount the first week in February, 1955.

For Jimmy it was going home. But it was also the realization that the meteoric rise to fame that had already begun that night in Santa Monica had cut him off forever from his small-town Midwestern origins, and that he could never really go home again. Still, in those bitter-cold, late-winter days, as Jimmy and I roamed the town and farm and fields of Fairmount, visiting family and friends, I came to know, or at least to glimpse, the real James Dean.

FAIRMOUNT, INDIANA

When we arrived at Fairmount, Indiana, shooting on *East of Eden* had been completed, but the film had not yet been released. Still, the townspeople sensed that James Dean was somebody special. The local papers had followed his blooming career; he had already appeared on television. But as yet no one suspected the full proportions his fame would assume.

In the streets of Fairmount.

Jimmy's return to Fairmount was more than a mere visit. With the completion of *East of Eden* Jimmy had experienced Hollywood and the intimations of stardom. At this point he was straddling two worlds – the world of his origins in Fairmount and the early stages of stardom – and he knew instinctively that the two were in conflict. And so he went back to Fairmount, to examine his origins and to preserve what was relevant.

Talking to the locals.

February is a rough month in the Midwest – not the ideal time to observe anything, much less to probe your past. It is a lean, grey time, and that is the mood, too. But maybe this was part of Jimmy's constantly testing everything: nothing ought to be idyllic. As was so often the case with Jimmy, he seemed to stack the cards against himself.

With his cousin Markie and school friends.

The barnyard was a natural for Jimmy; he explored and performed in the pens, troughs, and barn, testing his past pleasures for their validity in the future. He appreciated the surreal aspects of our search and happily responded to the pigs' oinking accompaniment to the bongos, the sow's dignified pose for the portrait, and the blasé heifers' acceptance.

In the driveway to the farm owned by his uncle, Marcus Winslow.

Outside the barn with a goat.

Group scene with calves.

Group scene with calves.

Group scene with calves.

Jimmy carried his bongo drums with him wherever he went – to New York, to Hollywood, and home to Fairmount. He became more and more attached to them as he learned to play better, and, as we've seen, he tried them out on the barnyard animals.

A drum solo for the animals.

"Tintype with Sow." Why? There is no logic to it, at least no logic readily apparent to the two young men Jimmy and I were then. When we speak of a tintype we usually think of a portrait or a family image. And family means where we come from, what we belong to. It seems apparent to me now that here Jimmy was testing the simplest of things: do I belong to the animals – to the pigs, the cattle, the goats? Do they accept me? It soon became clear that the barnyard animals easily accepted Jimmy, and he them. Don't underestimate that tintype with sow! A sow can be ferocious, and doesn't easily lend itself to the pose you see here.

A drum solo for the animals.

"Tintype with Sow."

On the Winslows' farm.

On the Winslows' farm.

On the Winslows' farm.

If you want to get to your roots, you go into grave-yards, especially in a small town. One morning Jimmy, Markie and I wandered through Fairmount's Park Cemetery, which was filled with many Dean ancestors, and suddenly happened on the gravestone of Cal Dean, who I believe was an uncle or a great-uncle. Both Jimmy and I were struck by the odd coincidence of the name, for Jimmy, of course, had just finished portraying Cal Trask in *East of Eden*.

At the cemetery in Fairmount, by the grave of one of his ancestors.

Pushing Markie's Soap Box Derby Racer in
the yard.

Reading with cousin Markie.

Jimmy slid into a very simple and uncomplicated relationship with Markie – somewhat as an older brother might. While he was in Fairmount he helped Markie build a model Jaguar and repair his bicycle, and on occasion played with him in his improvised Soap Box Derby racer. I think Jimmy was seeing himself as a young boy: Markie's childhood was so much like his own, so intimately involved with the movement and power of tractors. And from that you move on to bikes and motorcycles and racing cars: the mechanical life. It was very easy for Jimmy to adapt almost immediately to that facet of the farm and, in that regard, to identify with his cousin.

Making a model car.

Jimmy's parents moved to California when he was six. Three years later, on July 14, 1940, his mother, Mildred Dean, died of cancer. His father, a dental technician, stayed on in California, but Jimmy was sent back to Indiana to be brought up by his aunt and uncle, Ortense and Marcus Winslow, in Fairmount, where Jimmy's grandparents also lived. It is probable that Jimmy never got over his mother's death, but it is nonetheless hard to imagine a better home, for a boy in such a situation, than the Winslows'. They were Quakers, and as Jimmy's grandmother Emma once said of them, "Both are wise and gentle. Their's is like a Quaker home should be. You never hear a harsh word there."

Jimmy's grandmother Emma Dean in his boyhood room.

Unknown to his family, Jimmy had a portable tape recorder with him, the microphone of which he had fastened to his wristwatch. He asked Charlie and Emma about his upbringing and his ancestors. One question they tried to settle was whom Jimmy had inherited his taste for acting from. The only thing Charlie could think of was that an ancestor of his had been an auctioneer. Probably the most decisive influence, which wasn't discussed, however, was that Jimmy's mother had played at theaters with him in his early childhood. She had built a stage, and together they performed plays of their own invention with small dolls.

Charlie Dean, Jimmy's grandfather.

Seated around the diningroom table in the
Winslows' farmhouse in Fairmount are
(clockwise) Jimmy, with back to camera;
Charlie Dean, Jimmy's grandfather; Marcus
Winslow, his uncle; Ortense Dean Winslow,
his aunt; grandmother Emma Dean; and
Markie, Jimmy's cousin.

Markie claps his hands over his ears at
Jimmy's bongo playing.

Jimmy in a real down-home pose, in his
long johns.

James Whitcomb Riley was the poet of the Hoosier, and Jimmy loved to read from his work, which he did one day for me after dinner, to give me a feeling of the people and place whence he had come.

We found an old Victrola in the basement
with some old 78s, and played them one
afternoon.

Jimmy repairing Markie's bicycle.

The Sweethearts' Ball was held on St. Valentine's Day, 1955. Since Jimmy was in town, he was invited, and he not only came but brought his bongo drums as well. During the evening he played with the band, and at one point gave a little speech. He was at that time twenty-four, several years out of school, but most of that year's seniors remembered him, and now that word of his impending fame had reached Fairmount, requests for autographs seemed appropriate.

At the Sweethearts' Ball at his old school, St. Valentine's Day, February 14, 1955.

At the Sweethearts' Ball.

At the Sweethearts' Ball.

At the Sweethearts' Ball.

At the Sweethearts' Ball.

Jimmy on the stage where he first performed.

In the old school house.

In the old school house.

The old classroom.

Reading in the hayloft.

Jimmy poses playfully in a coffin at Hunt's
Funeral Parlor in Fairmount. His own corpse
would be taken there seven months later.

Jimmy with his uncle, Charlie Knowland.

In Martin Carter's motorcycle shop, where
Jimmy bought his first motorbike.

NEW YORK

Times Square. Jimmy haunted it. For a novice actor, in the fifties, New York was the place to go. The theater was thriving, and television was alive and well. The Actors Studio, directed by Lee Strasberg, was in its heyday. So when James Whitmore, Jimmy's first drama coach in Los Angeles, said to him, "Go East, young man," he went. And in many ways, Jimmy felt more at home in New York than in Los Angeles.

In Times Square.

Portrait study.

Portrait study.

Portrait study.

Near Times Square.

We used to roam the streets of New York together, and I liked to photograph Jimmy observing others. He had a great natural curiosity about people, was a collector of street vignettes, and I was forever amazed at the oddities he would stumble on to. One of the oddest was Jimmy's passing a store one day and pausing to see what one of the two little girls had in her hand. What was it? A chicken head. Only Jimmy would happen upon such surreal situations.

We were walking down Sixth Avenue and
suddenly Jimmy spied a furniture store near
Rockefeller Center. "Performers are always
being looked at," he said. "I wonder what it
feels like to be inside and look out. Stay outside and photograph people's reaction to
me just sitting there staring out...." How did
people react? Most did notice him but then
moved on. The point is, few people did react:
this is New York, and the tempo of the city
in the fifties was just about as fast as it is
today. In a small town things would have
been different, but in New York...

Jimmy's apartment on Sixty-eighth Street just off Central Park West was small and stateroom-like, on the top floor – probably a maid's room in earlier days. It was crammed with books and records. Jimmy had a need to be surrounded with books, but I'm not sure he was a real reader. As for his interest in music, he once boasted, "I collect everything from twelfth- and thirteenth-century music to the extreme moderns – you know, Schönberg, Berg, Stravinsky. I also like Sinatra's 'Songs for Young Lovers' album."

Jimmy in his apartment on West 68th Street.

Jimmy in his apartment.

Jimmy in his apartment.

Jimmy's bookcase.

A lot of Jimmy's books had to do with the theater, of course, but note also Kafka, *I Go Pogo*, *Charlotte's Web*, Thomas Mann's *Death in Venice*, and, lower right, *Los Toros*. A minister in Fairmount had turned him onto bullfighting, an interest reflected as well in the horns and cape on the wall. I don't know whether Jimmy actually ever saw a bullfight, but he played a lot with that cape – fantasized, I suppose. There was something bull-like about Jimmy – testy, untamed, aggressive.

With the opening of *East of Eden*, Jimmy not only became an overnight celebrity but also had to assume many of the obligations and responsibilities that new role implied. Here, Jane Deacy and an accountant go over business with Jimmy, who tries to cope, but...

In the office of his agent, Jane Deacy, in New York.

In Jane Deacy's office, New York.

In Jane Deacy's office, New York.

Visibly bored...finally solves the problem by
putting his feet up and going to sleep.

Howard Thompson, of THE NEW YORK TIMES,
interviewing Jimmy at the apartment of his
East Coast agent, Jane Deacy, just after EAST
OF EDEN had opened at the Astor Theatre in
New York.

Jerry's Bar on West Fifty-fourth Street, across from the old Ziegfeld Theatre, was one of Jimmy's favorite New York hangouts. Don't assume he's passed out because he's had too much beer. Jimmy was an insomniac – the worst I've ever met – so at odd times and in odd places he would simply pass out, for a few minutes or a few hours, then wake up and set out again. He lived like a stray animal; in fact, come to think of it, he *was* a stray animal. He had a couple of favorite spots on the East Coast, and two or three more on the West Coast. In New York he kept his fifth-floor walk-up apartment on West Sixty-eighth Street, but since he couldn't sleep, he spent relatively little time there.

With a girlfriend in Jerry's Bar.

It seems that Jimmy's life in New York revolved around a very narrow area of a few blocks, the center of which was Times Square. I've often speculated that Jimmy's preoccupation with the drums was more an interest in sound than in the instrument itself; drums, motorcycles, sports cars – all vibrated with a powerful sound to which he responded.

Drum tuition with Cyril Jackson in a studio near Times Square.

Drum tuition with Cyril Jackson.

Drum tuition with Cyril Jackson.

Jimmy had attended Lee Strasberg's classes at The Actors Studio before Elia Kazan selected him to play Cal in *East of Eden*. ("Dean *is* Cal," Kazan is reported to have said after seeing Jimmy, and John Steinbeck was quick to agree.) Whenever Jimmy came back to New York, he would renew his links with The Actors Studio. Careful observers will doubtless be able to pick out of this 1955 photograph several other actors who subsequently went on to fame and fortune. This is a rare picture in every sense of the term, for Strasberg almost never let anyone photograph his classes.

A class at the Actors Studio. Jimmy is in the front row, third from the right.

Jimmy's insomnia posed a special problem for me; *LIFE* had assigned me to do a possible cover of Jimmy, and I made several appointments to shoot him. Sometimes he didn't show up at all, and when he did, he'd look like utter hell – a two- or three-day growth of beard, and enormous bags under his eyes. He was only twenty-four, but the effects of his lifestyle were already beginning to show.

In a bar at closing time.

In Geraldine Page's dressing room.

Jimmy and Geraldine Page were good friends, and they used to get together often to talk shop, or just for small talk. Note that in the picture on the left Geraldine has a clipping of Jimmy – a pre-release article on *East of Eden* – hanging on her dressing-room mirror.

With Geraldine Page in a bar.

He was not at all fastidious about his looks: in fact, he would turn up more often than not in shaggy-dog style at meetings both formal and informal. What prompted him to walk into this barber shop near Times Square one day when we were out walking I cannot say.

In the barber shop near Times Square.

In the barber shop near Times Square.

In the barber shop near Times Square.

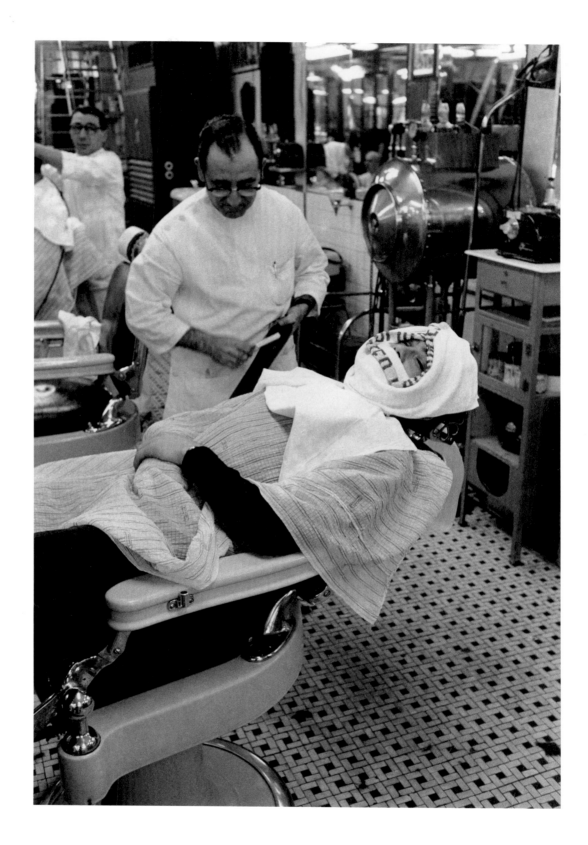

In the barber shop near Times Square.

Jimmy also studied dance as part of his actor's training. I am tempted to say this shows how seriously Jimmy took his art, which he did, but the fact is he was a dabbler: the bongo drums, African jazz, dance. Here he works out in Katherine Dunham's class, which was where he met Eartha Kitt.

In Katherine Dunham's dance class.

In Katherine Dunham's dance class.

In Katherine Dunham's dance class.

In Katherine Dunham's dance class.

In Katherine Dunham's dance class.

After *East of Eden*, Jimmy had a long-term nine-picture contract with Warner. More and more, he saw, California would necessarily be his home base. But whenever he could, he would sneak back to New York, "to life and the living of it," as he put it. One of his great pleasures in New York was to join Eartha Kitt in one of her dance classes, or to repair with her afterwards to a bar to talk.

In the dance group with Eartha Kitt.

In a bar with Eartha Kitt.

East of Eden opened in New York at the Astor Theatre, at Forty-fifth and Broadway, on March 10, after a celebrity-studded preview the night before as a benefit for The Actors Studio. But Jimmy was at neither the preview nor the opening. "I'm sorry," he had told Jane Deacy, "I can't handle that scene," and so he boarded a plane for L.A.

Flying back to California for the shooting of
REBEL WITHOUT A CAUSE.

HOLLYWOOD

Back in Hollywood, Jimmy tried to resume old routines, but a combination of his instantaneous fame and his own quirky, complicated personality made that difficult. He still hung out at Googie's, but anonymity, even there, was a thing of the past. Meanwhile he was preparing to film *Rebel Without a Cause*, which Nicholas Ray had persuaded Warner Brothers to make after the property had languished on their shelves for seven years. It was the first movie of the new nine-film contract.

Now poverty was a thing of the past, and with ready cash available, and credit no problem, Jimmy began buying bigger and faster racing cars. He made no bones about it with the studio executives that racing interested him far more than acting, a statement that obviously failed to endear him to them, for two reasons: it was an affront to their corporate and creative dignity; and they felt the damn kid would end up getting hurt, thus endangering their investment on any film in progress. Jimmy's latest acquisition was a four-thousand-dollar Porsche Speedster, which in the spring of 1955 he entered in a race at Palm Springs. He not only won in the amateur class but came in third among the professional drivers, and this only whetted his appetite for more and better races.

He was still insomniac, and night after night he would stay up driving, or drinking, with local cronies or with friends from back home who would come to visit. But no matter how late he stayed up, somehow he usually managed to make it to the set on time. There were exceptions, of course, with which Hollywood legend abounds, but in my experience, when Jimmy held up shooting, or showed up late, it was usually because he was at odds with the studio; it was his way of scoring a point for what he considered to be justice.

James Dean's Hollywood career was brilliant and brief. *East of Eden* opened, as we have seen, in March, 1955. *Rebel* finished shooting in June, 1955. From *Rebel*, Jimmy moved directly to *Giant*, which finished shooting in September of the same year. Before the month was out, Jimmy was dead.

During the shooting of REBEL WITHOUT
A CAUSE.

Still from REBEL WITHOUT A CAUSE.

Still from REBEL WITHOUT A CAUSE.

The famous knife-fight from REBEL WITHOUT
A CAUSE.

The famous knife-fight from REBEL WITHOUT
A CAUSE.

In a scene from the television play THE
DARK, DARK HOUSE with Ronald Reagan.

114

"There really isn't an opportunity for greatness in this world. We are impaled on a crock of conditioning. A fish that is in water has no choice that he is. Genius would have it that he swim in sand.... We are fish and we drown." James Dean

Jimmy on the studio lot in Hollywood.

"If a choice is in order – I'd rather have people hiss than yawn. Any public figure sets himself up as a target and that is the chance he takes. Most of us have more than one choice and I chose to be what I am, rather than remain a farm boy back in Indiana.... Despite the endless odds and issues along the way, I've never regretted it." James Dean

Jimmy on the studio lot in Hollywood.